Introduction

Welcome to the exhilarating world of travel hacking, where adventure and savings have a baby! Prepare to embark on a journey filled with ingenious strategies, secret shortcuts, and surprising tips that will transform the way you explore and travel the globe. Imagine unlocking the hidden treasure chest of insider knowledge about a certain topic, where every step you take is a well-calculated leap towards unforgettable experiences and extraordinary savings. Whether you're a seasoned globetrotter seeking to magnify your travel prowess or a curious wanderer eager to unleash your inner Goonies, this book is your skeleton key to unlocking a realm of travel hacking magic.

 In these pages, you'll discover a treasure map of travel hacks that will blow you away to breathtaking destinations while keeping your wallet geeking (that's happy) . From unraveling the enigma of finding the cheapest flights to discovering the best-kept secrets of accommodation savings, to bringing you the most innovative and entertaining strategies that will leave you awe-inspired. But this isn't your ordinary travel guide; it's an Unordinary adventure in itself.

Prepare to percolate *no pun intended* into a world where packing becomes an art form, dining becomes a culinary voyage, and sightseeing transforms into a symphony of discovery and bliss. This book is up to date as of 2023. We'll show you how to tap into the local pulse of a destination, connect with fellow adventurers, and create memories that will forever be etched in your mind and heart.

So fasten your seatbelts, fellow wanderers, and get ready for a rollercoaster ride through the realm of travel hacking. Let your imagination soar as we unravel the secrets, debunk the myths, and empower you to embark on the best journeys of your life—all while saving money, making unforgettable memories, and embracing the bliss of being a travel hacker.

Adventure awaits, my friend. It's time to turn the key and open the doors to a world where travel dreams become a thrilling reality. Let's set sail together on this epic voyage of discovery and create travel stories that will be whispered with awe around campfires for years to come. Are you ready to become the master of your own travel destiny? Let the travel hacking adventure begin!

This A Good Jawn.

Photo Credit To UI Visualz

Tables Of Content

Chapter 1: Planning and Booking Tips - 15

Chapter 2: Transportation and Getting Around - 20

Chapter 9: Local Experiences and Activities Hacks - 97

Chapter 1

Planning and Booking Tips

1.1 Adaptable Travel Dates

Being adaptable with your movement dates can assist you with tracking down critical limits on flights and facilities. Aircrafts and lodgings frequently change their costs in view of interest, so going during off-top seasons or keeping away from occasions can prompt significant reserve funds.

1.2 Incognito Mode

When searching for flights or hotels online, use your browser's incognito mode or clear your cookies. Travel websites may use dynamic pricing, which means they can adjust prices based on your search history and demand. By using incognito mode, you can prevent websites from tracking your search activity, potentially leading to lower prices.

1.3 Set Notification Alerts

Set fare alerts from travel websites or apps to receive notifications when prices drop for your desired destinations.

1.4 Off-Peak Travel

Traveling during off-peak seasons can offer significant cost savings and a more enjoyable experience with fewer crowds. Research the shoulder seasons or less popular months for your desired destinations. Not only will you find better deals on flights and accommodations, but you'll also have a chance to explore attractions without the overwhelming crowds often seen during peak periods.

1.5 Booking in Advance

Booking in advance can often result in better prices and more availability, especially for popular attractions or activities. By planning ahead, you can secure discounted rates and avoid last-minute price increases. This applies not only to flights and accommodations but also to tours, theater tickets, and other experiences. Check the cancellation policies before booking to guarantee flexibility in case your plans change.

1.6 Package Deals

Consider booking package deals that combine flights, accommodations, and sometimes additional services like car rentals or tours. Package deals can offer better overall pricing compared to booking each component separately. Look for deals on travel websites or directly through airlines and hotels. However, compare the prices with individual bookings to ensure you're getting the best value.

1.7 Alternate Airports

When searching for flights, consider checking prices from nearby airports. Sometimes, flying into or out of a different airport can lead to substantial savings. Research transportation options between airports and your final destination to evaluate if the cost and convenience outweigh the potential savings.

1.8 Loyalty Programs and Memberships

Joining loyalty programs for airlines, hotels, or car rental companies can provide numerous benefits. These programs often offer exclusive discounts, rewards points, upgrades, and other perks. Accumulating points through loyalty programs can result in free flights, hotel stays, or other discounts in the future. Additionally, membership programs like AAA or AARP may provide special rates or additional benefits for travelers.

1.9 Research Visa and Entry Requirements

Before planning an international trip, familiarize yourself with the visa and entry requirements necessary for your destination. Some countries have specific visa regulations or entry fees that may impact your travel costs. Plan accordingly and factor in these expenses when budgeting for your trip.

1.10 Consult Travel Forums and Blogs

Take advantage of travel forums and blogs where experienced travelers share tips, tricks, and advice. These platforms often provide insider information on how to find the best deals, discounts, and hidden gems in various destinations. Engaging with the travel community can offer valuable insights and help you save money during your trip.

(Remember, the key to planning and booking effectively is research and flexibility. By implementing these tips, you can optimize your travel budget and find the best deals.)

1.11 Consider Alternative Accommodations

In addition to traditional hotels, consider alternative accommodations such as vacation rentals, guesthouses, or hostels. These options often offer lower prices compared to hotels, especially for longer stays or when traveling with a group. Websites and apps like Airbnb, Vrbo, or Hostelworld allow you to explore a wide range of alternative accommodations and compare prices.

1.12 Use Price Comparison Websites

Utilize price comparison websites to seek the best deals and offers on flights, hotels, and rental cars. Websites like Kayak, hopper, or Google Flights that allows you to compare prices from multiple airlines and travel agencies, ensuring that you get the most competitive rates. Additionally, consider using hotel-specific search engines or aggregator sites that compile prices from various booking platforms.

1.13 Take Advantage of Travel Rewards Credit Cards

Consider applying for a travel rewards credit card that offers benefits like airline miles, hotel points, or cashback on traveling -related expenses. These cards often come with sign-up bonuses and reward points for everyday spending, which can be redeemed for discounted or free flights, hotel stays, or other travel expenses. However, make sure to use credit cards responsibly and pay off the balance on them in full each month until it's paid off to avoid interest charges.

1.14 Research Local Transportation Options

Before your trip, research the local transportation options available at your destination. Utilize public transportation like buses, trains, or trams, which are often more affordable than taxis or rental cars. Look for multi-day or unlimited travel passes that offer discounted rates for frequent use. Additionally, consider walking or cycling in areas where it's safe and convenient, as it not only saves money but also allows you to experience the destination in a unique way.

1.15 Explore Free and Low-Cost Activities

Research and prioritize free or low-cost activities and attractions at your destination. Many cities offer free walking tours, public parks, museums with discounted or free admission on certain days, and cultural events that provide a rich experience without breaking the bank. Look for local festivals, markets, or street performances where you can immerse yourself in the local culture without spending a fortune.

1.16 Travel with a Group

Consider traveling with a group of friends or family members to split costs. Group bookings often come with discounts on accommodations, tours, and even group airfare rates. Sharing expenses like transportation, accommodations, and meals can significantly reduce individual costs, allowing you to enjoy more activities without overspending.

1.17 Utilize Travel Apps and Websites

Make use of travel apps and websites that aggregate discounts, deals, and coupons for various aspects of your trip. Apps like TripIt, Hopper, or Travelzoo provide access to exclusive promotions, discounted activities, and limited-time offers. Subscribe to newsletters and follow travel deal websites or social media accounts that curate and share the latest discounts and promotions in the travel industry.

1.18 Check for Hidden Fees

When booking flights, accommodations, or car rentals, be mindful of hidden fees that may inflate the final cost. Read the fine print and understand the terms and conditions associated with your bookings. Pay attention to additional charges like baggage fees, resort fees, parking fees, or credit card surcharges. Being aware of these fees allows you to factor them into your budget or explore alternatives to avoid unnecessary expenses.

1.19 Use Local Tourism Offices or Visitor Centers

Visit local tourism offices or visitor centers upon arrival at your destination. These establishments often provide maps, brochures, and valuable information on local attractions, discounts, and special offers. The staff can offer advice on budget-friendly activities, recommend affordable dining options, and provide insights into hidden gems or lesser-known attractions that can enhance your travel experience.

1.20 Be Open to Spontaneity and Flexibility

While planning is quite important, leaving room for spontaneity and flexibility can lead to unexpected savings. Keep an open mind and be willing to collect opportunities that may arise during your trip. Last-minute deals on accommodations, tours, or activities can often be found, especially during off-peak periods. By being flexible with your itinerary, you can take advantage of these offers and potentially save money while enjoying unique experiences.

1.21 Avoid Overpacking

Packing light can save you money and make your travels more convenient. Airlines often charge extra fees for overweight or oversized luggage, so pack efficiently to avoid these additional expenses. Research the baggage allowance for your airline and destination, and only pack what you truly need. Consider versatile clothing items that can be mixed and matched, and bring travel-sized toiletries to save space and weight.

1.22 Research Dining Options

Eating out can quickly become a pocket killer while traveling. Research affordable dining options such as local eateries, food markets, or street food vendors that offer delicious and budget-friendly meals. Ask locals for recommendations on where to find authentic and reasonably priced cuisine. Additionally, consider self-catering options by booking accommodations with kitchenettes, allowing you to prepare some meals yourself and save on dining expenses.

1.23 Explore Alternative Airline Routes

When booking flights, consider exploring alternative routes to your destination. Sometimes, flying with layovers or connecting flights can be cheaper than direct routes. Use flight search engines that allow you to compare different itineraries and airlines to find the most affordable option. However, ensure you have ample time for connections and take into account the potential inconveniences of longer travel times.

1.24 Research and Compare Travel Insurance Options

Travel insurance is essential for protecting yourself against unexpected expenses and fees, such as trip cancellations, medical emergencies, or lost luggage. However, insurance policies can vary in terms of coverage, cost, and exclusions.

Research and compare different travel insurance options to find one that suits your needs and budget. Consider factors such as coverage limits, deductibles, and emergency assistance services.

1.25 Utilize Student or Senior Discounts

If you're a student or a senior, take advantage of the discounts available to you. Many attractions, museums, transportation services, and even accommodation providers offer discounted rates for students or seniors. Carry your student or senior identification cards with you and inquire about any available discounts when making bookings or purchasing tickets.

1.26 Follow Airlines and Travel

Companies and agencies on social media stay updated on the latest deals and promotions by following airlines, hotels, and travel companies on social media platforms. They often announce flash sales, limited-time offers, or exclusive discounts through their social media channels. By being connected, you can be among the first to know about these deals and secure significant savings on flights, accommodations, or travel packages.

1.27 Consider House Sitting or Home Exchange

House sitting or home exchange programs offer opportunities to stay in accommodations for free or at a significantly reduced cost. Websites like TrustedHousesitters or HomeExchange connect travelers with homeowners who need someone to look after their properties or exchange homes for a set period. These options not only save you money on accommodations but also provide a unique and immersive travel experience.

1.28 Take Advantage of Free Walking Tours

Many cities around the world offer free walking tours led by local guides who provide insights into the city's history, culture, and landmarks. Joining these tours not only gives you a chance to explore the destination on foot but also allows you to learn from knowledgeable guides at no cost. While the tours are free, it's customary to tip the guide based on your satisfaction.

1.29 Check for Group Discounts or Travel Packages

If you're traveling with a group of friends, family, or colleagues, inquire about group discounts or travel packages. Many attractions, tours, and accommodations offer special rates for larger groups. Contact the providers directly to negotiate group rates or check their websites for any available group packages. By pooling your resources and booking as a group, you can enjoy significant savings on various aspects of your trip.

1.30 Research Local Events and Festivals

Research local events, festivals, or cultural celebrations happening during your travel dates. These events often showcase the destination's unique traditions, music, dance, and culinary delights. Attending such events can provide memorable experiences at little to no cost, as many festivals have free entry or offer affordable tickets for cultural performances and exhibitions.

1.31 Visit Tourist Information Centers

Visit tourist information centers or visitor bureaus at your destination. These centers often provide maps, brochures, and valuable insights into local attractions, discounts, and special offers. The staff can offer advice on budget-friendly activities, recommend affordable dining options, and provide up-to-date information on current promotions or discounted tickets for popular attractions.

1.32 Explore Volunteering Opportunities

Consider participating in volunteering opportunities during your travels. Many organizations around the world offer volunteer programs where you can contribute your skills, time, or expertise to meaningful projects. In exchange for your help, you may receive free or heavily discounted accommodations, meals, or even local transportation. Volunteering not only allows you to give back to the community but also provides an affordable way to explore a destination.

1.33 Opt for Day Trips or Excursions from Base Locations

Instead of booking separate accommodations for every destination, consider selecting a central base location and taking day trips or excursions to nearby attractions. This approach allows you to save on accommodation costs while still exploring multiple places. Research public transportation options or join organized tours that depart from your base location, and plan your itinerary accordingly.

1.34 Consider Traveling in a Group Tour

Group tours can be an efficient and cost-effective way to explore a destination, especially if you're visiting a region with complex logistics or limited public transportation options. Group tours often include transportation, accommodations, and guided activities, and they can offer group discounts due to bulk bookings. Research reputable tour operators and compare prices to find group tours that suit your interests and budget.

1.35 Be Mindful of Overtourism

In popular tourist destinations, over tourism can lead to inflated prices, crowded attractions, and a strain on local resources. Consider visiting lesser-known or off-the-beaten-path destinations to experience authentic culture, lower prices, and fewer crowds. Not only will you save money, but you'll also contribute to more sustainable and responsible tourism practices.

(Remember, every traveler's needs and preferences are unique. Adapt these planning and booking tips to suit your specific travel goals, budget, and comfort level. With careful research, flexibility, and a willingness to explore alternative options, you can make the most of your travel budget and create unforgettable experiences.)

Chapter 2:

Transportation and Getting Around

2.1 Research Different Transportation Options

When traveling, research and compare different transportation options available at your destination. Depending on the location, you may have choices such as trains, buses, taxis, rideshares, ferries, or even bicycles. Consider factors like cost, convenience, safety, and the local transportation system's reliability to determine the best mode of transport for each leg of your journey.

2.2 Public Transportation Passes

Many cities and regions offer public transportation passes or cards that provide unlimited travel for a set period. These passes are often more cost-effective than purchasing individual tickets for each journey. Research and compare the available passes, such as daily, weekly, or monthly options, and evaluate if they align with your planned itinerary. Public transportation passes can save you money while allowing you to navigate the destination conveniently.

2.3 Walk or Cycle Whenever Possible

Exploring a city on foot or by bicycle not only saves money but also allows you to immerse yourself in the local culture and discover hidden gems. Many cities have well-designed pedestrian areas or dedicated cycling lanes. Use maps or mobile apps to plan walking routes or find bike-sharing services. Walking or cycling can also contribute to a healthier and more sustainable travel experience.

2.4 Carpooling or Ride-Sharing Services

Consider carpooling or using ride-sharing services like Uber or Lyft to share transportation costs with other travelers or locals heading in the same direction. Carpooling can be a cost-effective and social way to travel, especially for longer distances or when public transportation options are limited. Connect with fellow travelers through online platforms or social media groups to find potential carpooling opportunities.

2.5 Off-Peak Travel for Flights

When booking flights, consider flying during off-peak hours or days. Early morning or late-night flights tend to be less expensive compared to peak travel times. Additionally, midweek flights are often cheaper than those on weekends when demand is higher. Being flexible with your departure and arrival times can help you secure more affordable airfare options.

2.6 Use Flight Comparison Websites

Utilize flight comparison websites to find the best deals on airfare. Websites like Skyscanner, Kayak, or Google Flights allow you to search for flights across multiple airlines, compare prices, and filter results based on your preferences. Set up price alerts to be notified when fares for your desired routes drop. Additionally, consider booking flights directly with airlines, as they may offer exclusive promotions or discounts.

2.7 Consider Budget Airlines

Budget airlines often offer lower fares compared to full-service carriers. Research and compare the offerings of different budget airlines in your region. Keep in mind that budget airlines may have additional fees for services like checked baggage, seat selection, or in-flight meals. Read the terms and conditions carefully and calculate the total cost, including any additional charges, to ensure that the budget airline option is indeed the most cost-effective choice.

2.8 Travel by Train or Bus

In certain regions, traveling by train or bus can be a more affordable option compared to flying, especially for shorter distances. Research regional train or bus networks, and compare prices and travel times. Train or bus travel often offers scenic views and allows you to experience the local landscape and culture up close.

2.9 Renting a Car

If you plan to explore a destination extensively or visit remote areas where public transportation is limited, renting a car may be a suitable option. Research different car rental companies, compare prices, and read reviews to find a reputable and affordable option. Consider factors like fuel efficiency, insurance coverage, and any additional fees associated with renting a car. Book in advance to secure better rates and availability.

2.10 Be Mindful of Peak Travel Times

During peak travel seasons or holidays, transportation prices tend to be higher due to increased demand. If possible, avoid traveling during these peak periods to secure better rates. Consider visiting destinations during shoulder seasons or off-peak times when prices are generally lower. Not only will you save money on transportation, but you'll also encounter fewer crowds and enjoy a more relaxed travel experience.

2.11 Research and Compare Airport Transportation Options

When arriving at an airport, research the available transportation options to your accommodation. Compare the prices of taxis, private transfers, shuttle services, or public transportation. Consider factors like convenience, cost, and travel time. In some cases, public transportation may be the most cost-effective option, while in others, a pre-booked transfer or shuttle service might be more convenient, especially if you're traveling with heavy luggage or arriving late at night.

2.12 Take Advantage of Free City Shuttles

Some cities offer free shuttle services that transport passengers between major tourist attractions or specific areas. These shuttles are often funded by local governments or tourism boards as a way to encourage visitors to explore the city and reduce congestion. Research if your destination offers any free shuttle services, and take advantage of them to save money on transportation while conveniently accessing key attractions.

2.13 Negotiate with Local Transportation Providers

In certain destinations, particularly in developing countries or areas with informal transportation systems, you may have the opportunity to negotiate fares with local drivers or transportation providers. Be respectful and friendly while negotiating, and ensure that the agreed-upon price is fair and reasonable. Bargaining can be an effective way to secure lower transportation costs, particularly for short trips or private hires.

2.14 Consider Multi-Stop or Open-Jaw Flights

If your travel plans involve visiting multiple destinations or returning from a different city than where you arrived, consider booking multi-stop or open-jaw flights. These options allow you to visit multiple cities without having to purchase separate one-way tickets. Comparing prices for different flight combinations can help you find the most cost-effective route for your itinerary.

2.15 Check for Parking Options and Fees

If you're renting a car or driving your own vehicle, research the parking options and associated fees at your destination. In some cities, parking fees can be exorbitant, particularly in touristy areas or city centers. Look for affordable parking garages, street parking regulations, or even free parking zones outside the city center. Planning ahead and being aware of parking options can save you money and potential parking fines.

2.16 Learn Basic Local Phrases for Transportation

Learning a few basic phrases in the local language can be helpful when using public transportation or communicating with drivers. Knowing how to ask for directions, inquire about fares, or confirm drop-off points can make your travel experience smoother and potentially prevent misunderstandings. Locals often appreciate the effort, which might even lead to better customer service or helpful advice.

2.17 Check for Student or Senior Transportation Discounts

If you're a student or senior, check if your destination offers discounted transportation fares for these demographics. Many cities, regions, or transportation providers provide special rates for students or seniors. Carry your identification card or relevant documentation, and inquire about any available discounts when purchasing tickets or using public transportation. Taking advantage of these discounts can result in significant savings.

2.18 Research and Compare Car Rental Insurance Options

When renting a car, it's important to consider insurance coverage. Car rental companies typically offer additional insurance options, but these can significantly increase the overall cost. Research your existing car insurance policy, credit card benefits, or independent travel insurance coverage to determine if you're already protected for car rentals. Understanding your insurance options can help you avoid unnecessary expenses and make an informed decision.

2.19 Check for Student or Senior Transportation Discounts

If you're a student or senior, check if your destination offers discounted transportation fares for these demographics. Many cities, regions, or transportation providers provide special rates for students or seniors. Carry your Identification card or relevant documentation, and inquire about any available discounts when purchasing tickets or using public transportation. Taking advantage of these discounts can result in significant savings.

2.20 Research and Compare Car Rental Insurance Options

When renting a car, it's important to consider insurance coverage. Car rental companies typically offer additional insurance options, but these can significantly increase the overall cost. Research your existing car insurance policy, credit card benefits, or independent travel insurance coverage to determine if you're already protected for car rentals. Understanding your insurance options can help you avoid unnecessary expenses and make an informed decision.

2.21 Use Travel Apps and Mobile Tickets

Make use of travel apps and mobile tickets to streamline your transportation experience. Many cities have their own transportation apps that provide real-time information on routes, schedules, and fare payments. These apps often offer mobile ticketing options, allowing you to purchase and display tickets directly on your smartphone. Using travel apps and mobile tickets can save you time, reduce the need for physical tickets, and sometimes even offer exclusive discounts or promotions.

2.22 Consider Alternative Transportation Modes

Think outside the box when it comes to transportation. Depending on the destination and local infrastructure, consider alternative modes of transportation such as tuk-tuks, rickshaws, cable cars, or even horse-drawn carriages. These modes may not be the most practical for all situations, but they can provide unique experiences while potentially saving you money compared to traditional options.

2.23 Use Frequent Flyer or Rewards Programs

If you frequently travel by air, consider joining frequent flyer programs or airline rewards programs. Accumulating miles or points through these programs can lead to discounted or free flights in the future. Take advantage of credit cards that offer travel rewards and consider consolidating your travel expenses to earn more points. Be mindful of program rules, expiration dates, and any associated fees to maximize the benefits.

2.24 Plan Layovers Strategically

When booking flights with layovers, plan them strategically to save on transportation costs. If there's a long layover in a city, consider taking advantage of it to explore the destination. Some airlines offer free city tours or discounted transportation for passengers with long layovers. Research if your layover city offers such programs, and use the opportunity to see a new place without additional travel expenses.

2.25 Share Transportation Costs with Travel Companions

If you're traveling with friends, family, or fellow travelers, split transportation costs to reduce individual expenses. Share the costs of taxis, ride-shares, or even rental cars. Coordinate your travel plans and calculate the total expenses, then divide them among the group. This way, everyone can contribute their fair share, making transportation more affordable for all.

2.26 Stay Flexible with Transportation Options

Maintain flexibility with your transportation choices, especially if you're seeking the best deals. Consider alternative airports or train stations nearby, as they may offer lower fares or better options. Be open to adjusting your travel dates or times if it means securing cheaper transportation. Staying flexible allows you to take advantage of sudden discounts, promotions, or last-minute deals.

2.27 Avoid Excess Baggage Fees

To avoid excess baggage fees, pack light and be mindful of weight restrictions imposed by airlines or transportation providers. Research the baggage allowances in advance and pack accordingly. Consider using compression bags or packing cubes to optimize space and minimize the need for additional luggage. If necessary, wear your heavier or bulkier items during travel to reduce the weight of your checked baggage.

2.28 Be Aware of Local Transportation Etiquette

Every destination has its own transportation etiquette and customs. Research and familiarize yourself with the local norms to ensure a smooth and respectful experience. Understand how to queue for buses or trains, when to offer seats to others, and how to interact with drivers or fellow passengers. Adhering to local etiquette can help you blend in, avoid misunderstandings, and create positive interactions during your travels.

(Remember, these transportation and getting around tips are meant to provide general guidance. Always research and adapt them to the specific destination and circumstances of your trip. By being resourceful, flexible, and mindful of your budget, you can make the most of your transportation options and enjoy a seamless travel experience.)

Chapter 3:

Accommodation and Lodging

3.1 Research Accommodation Options

When planning your trip, thoroughly research different accommodation options available at your destination. Explore a range of choices, including hotels, hostels, guesthouses, vacation rentals, bed and breakfasts, and even unique accommodations like farm stays or eco-lodges. Consider factors such as location, amenities, reviews, and pricing to find the best accommodation that suits your preferences and budget.

3.2 Compare Prices on Multiple Platforms

To find the best deals on accommodation, compare prices on multiple platforms. Use hotel comparison websites like Booking.com, Expedia, or Kayak to compare rates across different booking sites. Additionally, check the hotel's official website, as they may offer exclusive promotions or discounts. By comparing prices, you can ensure that you're getting the best possible rate for your chosen accommodation.

3.3 Book in Advance

Booking your accommodation in advance can often lead to better prices and more options. Popular hotels and highly-rated properties tend to fill up quickly, so securing your reservation early ensures you have a wider selection. Additionally, some hotels offer early bird discounts or special rates for advanced bookings. Plan your itinerary in advance, and make your accommodation reservations accordingly.

3.4 Stay in Less Touristy Areas

Consider staying in less touristy areas to save on accommodation costs. Accommodation prices are typically higher in popular tourist districts, city centers, or near major attractions. By choosing accommodations in residential neighborhoods or outskirts, you may find more affordable options. Keep in mind accessibility to transportation and the safety of the area when selecting accommodation in less touristy areas.

3.5 Consider Alternative Accommodation Options

Think beyond traditional hotels and explore alternative accommodation options. Platforms like Airbnb, Vrbo, or HomeAway offer vacation rentals and private homes that can be more cost-effective, especially for families or larger groups. Additionally, consider house-sitting, couch-surfing, or volunteering programs that provide free or low-cost accommodation in exchange for services or assistance.

3.6 Stay Longer for Discounts

Some accommodations offer discounts or reduced rates for extended stays. If your travel plans allow, consider staying at the same accommodation for a longer duration to take advantage of these discounts. This can be particularly beneficial for slow-paced travel or when exploring a specific region in depth. Inquire about weekly or monthly rates when making your reservation.

3.7 Be Flexible with Travel Dates

Flexibility with travel dates can significantly impact accommodation prices. Avoid peak travel seasons or holidays when prices tend to be higher. Instead, consider traveling during off-peak periods or shoulder seasons when rates are lower. Additionally, midweek stays are often cheaper than weekends when hotels experience higher demand. Adjusting your travel dates by a few days can result in substantial savings on accommodation.

3.8 Consider Package Deals or Bundle Bookings

Package deals or bundle bookings that include both accommodation and transportation can offer cost savings. Some travel websites or tour operators offer package deals that combine flights, hotels, and sometimes even activities or tours. Evaluate if these package deals align with your travel plans and compare prices with individual bookings to ensure you're getting the best value for your money.

3.9 Join Loyalty Programs or Hotel Memberships

If you frequently travel or have a preferred hotel chain, consider joining loyalty programs or hotel memberships. These programs often provide exclusive discounts, rewards points, and member-only benefits. Accumulate points or take advantage of member rates to save on accommodation costs. Additionally, sign up for email newsletters or follow hotels on social media to receive notifications about special promotions or flash sales.

3.10 Consider Shared Accommodations

Shared accommodation options like hostels or dormitories can be significantly cheaper than private rooms. If you're comfortable with a shared space, consider staying in a hostel or budget guesthouse. Many hostels offer private rooms as well, providing a balance between privacy and affordability. Hostels also provide opportunities to meet fellow travelers, exchange travel tips, and participate in social activities.

3.11 Look for Last-Minute Deals

If you're flexible with your travel plans and can afford to wait until the last minute, consider looking for last-minute deals on accommodation. Websites and apps like HotelTonight specialize in offering discounted rates on unsold hotel rooms for same-day or next-day stays. Keep in mind that availability may be limited, and it's not guaranteed that you'll find suitable accommodation, especially during peak travel periods.

3.12 Utilize Price Match Guarantees

Many hotel booking websites offer price match guarantees, where they promise to match or beat a lower rate found on another platform. Take advantage of this by searching for the best available rates and then contacting the hotel or booking website to request a price match. By doing so, you can secure the lowest possible price for your chosen accommodation.

3.13 Consider Alternative Accommodation Experiences

To save money and have a unique experience, consider alternative accommodation experiences such as houseboats, treehouses, or camping. Depending on your destination, you might find opportunities to stay on a houseboat on a canal, sleep in a cozy treehouse in a forest, or camp in national parks. These alternative accommodation options often provide a more immersive and memorable travel experience

3.14 Negotiate Room Rates

In some situations, particularly when booking directly with smaller hotels or guesthouses, it may be possible to negotiate room rates. This is especially true if you're staying for an extended period or during the off-peak season. Politely inquire if there is any room for negotiation or if they can offer any additional perks or upgrades. While not always successful, it's worth a try to potentially secure a better deal.

3.15 Take Advantage of Hotel Amenities

When selecting accommodation, consider the amenities provided by the hotel. Some hotels offer complimentary breakfast, free Wi-Fi, access to fitness centers or swimming pools, or even shuttle services. While the initial room rate may be slightly higher, taking advantage of these amenities can save you money on meals, transportation, and entertainment.

3.16 Consider Homestays or Local Guesthouses

For a more immersive cultural experience, consider staying in homestays or local guesthouses. These options allow you to stay with local families or in smaller, family-run establishments. Not only can this be a more affordable option, but it also provides an opportunity to connect with locals, learn about their culture, and receive insider tips on the best places to visit and eat.

3.17 Book Refundable or Flexible Cancellation Policies

When making accommodation reservations, pay attention to the cancellation policies. Opt for rooms with flexible cancellation policies or book refundable rates. This gives you the flexibility to adjust your travel plans if needed without incurring unnecessary costs. However, always double-check the terms and conditions to understand any potential fees or restrictions associated with cancellations or modifications.

3.18 Avoid Additional Fees and Charges

Read the fine print and be aware of any additional fees or charges that may be imposed by the accommodation. Some hotels may charge for amenities like parking, Wi-Fi, or resort fees, which can significantly increase your overall cost. Look for accommodations that offer these services free of charge or consider alternative options to avoid unnecessary expenses.

3.19 Seek Local Recommendations and Reviews

Before finalizing your accommodation choice, seek local recommendations and read reviews from previous guests. Local recommendations can provide insights into lesser-known accommodations that may offer better value for money. Online reviews on platforms like TripAdvisor or Google can give you an idea of the overall guest experience, cleanliness, and customer service of the accommodation. Take note of both positive and negative reviews to make an informed decision.

3.20 Consider Long-Term Rentals or Apartment Shares

If you're planning an extended stay or traveling with a group, consider long-term rentals or apartment shares. Websites like Airbnb, HomeAway, or FlipKey offer options to rent apartments or houses for weeks or months at a time. These accommodations often come with kitchen facilities, allowing you to prepare your own meals and save money on dining out. Negotiate with the host for a discounted rate for long-term stays.

3.21 Use Price Tracking Tools

To ensure you get the best price for your accommodation, use price tracking tools or set up price alerts. Websites like Trivago or Google Flights allow you to set price alerts for specific accommodations or destinations. They will notify you when prices drop, enabling you to book at the optimal time to secure the lowest rates.

3.22 Check for Extra Perks or Discounts

Some accommodations offer additional perks or discounts that can enhance your stay and save you money. Look for accommodations that provide complimentary airport transfers, free meals for children, discounted spa treatments, or access to exclusive facilities. Take advantage of these extra perks to enhance your overall travel experience without increasing your expenses.

3.23 Consider Work Exchange or Volunteer Programs

If you're open to trading your skills or time for accommodation, consider work exchange or volunteer programs. Platforms like Workaway or HelpX connect travelers with hosts who offer accommodation in exchange for assistance with various tasks. This arrangement allows you to save money on accommodation while immersing yourself in local culture and contributing to meaningful projects.

3.24 Use Hotel Booking Apps for Exclusive Deals

Download hotel booking apps like Hotels.com, Booking.com, or Agoda to access exclusive deals and discounts. These apps often provide mobile-only offers, secret deals, or reward programs that can lead to further savings on accommodation. Take advantage of these apps to find discounted rates or earn rewards that can be redeemed for future bookings.

3.25 Consider Mid-Range or Budget Hotels

While luxury hotels may offer lavish amenities and services, they come with a higher price tag. Consider opting for mid-range or budget hotels that offer clean and comfortable accommodations without the hefty price. Look for hotels with positive reviews, convenient locations, and essential amenities to ensure a pleasant stay without overspending.

3.26 Stay on the Outskirts of Popular Destinations

If you're visiting a popular tourist destination, consider staying on the outskirts of the city or town. Accommodation prices tend to be lower in these areas, and you can often find good transportation connections to reach the main attractions. This strategy allows you to save on accommodation costs while still being within reach of the places you want to visit.

3.27 Contact the Accommodation Directly

Before making a reservation through a booking website, consider contacting the accommodation directly. Inquire about any available discounts, special offers, or upgrades. Sometimes, accommodations have unadvertised promotions or prefer direct bookings, which can lead to better rates or added benefits. By communicating directly, you can negotiate and secure the best deal possible.

(Remember to adapt these accommodation tips to suit your specific travel preferences, destination, and budget. By being proactive, flexible, and willing to explore different options, you can find affordable and comfortable accommodation that enhances your overall travel experience.)

Chapter 4:

<u>Dining and Restaurants</u>

4.1 Explore Local Food Markets

One of the best ways to experience the local cuisine and save money is by exploring local food markets. These markets offer a wide variety of fresh produce, local delicacies, and street food at affordable prices. Immerse yourself in the vibrant atmosphere, interact with local vendors, and indulge in authentic flavors while supporting the local economy.

4.2 Ask Locals for Restaurant Recommendations

When looking for dining options, don't hesitate to ask locals for their restaurant recommendations. Locals know the best hidden gems, local specialties, and affordable eateries that may not be listed in guidebooks or popular review websites. Strike up conversations with locals, hotel staff, or taxi drivers to get insider tips on where to find delicious and reasonably priced meals.

4.3 Embrace Street Food Culture

Street food is not only a delicious way to experience local flavors but also a budget-friendly option. Embrace the street food culture in your destination by trying popular street food dishes from food stalls or food trucks. Ensure the food is cooked fresh and looks hygienic, and follow the locals' lead when choosing which vendors to patronize. Street food is often a culinary adventure that offers a glimpse into the local food scene.

4.4 Set a Food Budget

To manage your dining expenses effectively, set a daily food budget. Determine how much you're willing to spend on meals each day and stick to that budget. Consider allocating more funds for special dining experiences or trying local delicacies while being mindful of cheaper meal options for the rest of your meals. This practice helps you prioritize your spending and avoid overspending on food.

4.5 Lunch Specials and Set Menus

Many restaurants offer lunch specials or set menus during specific hours of the day. Take advantage of these deals, as they often provide a more affordable way to enjoy a full meal compared to ordering à la carte during dinner. Look for restaurants that advertise lunch specials or ask the staff for any available set menus. This way, you can savor a satisfying meal at a lower price.

4.6 Explore Affordable Local Eateries

Venture beyond tourist areas to discover affordable local eateries. These neighborhood establishments often offer authentic dishes at reasonable prices. Look for places frequented by locals, as they tend to be more affordable than tourist-oriented restaurants. Check for local recommendations, read online reviews, or use food-focused apps to find hidden gems where you can enjoy delicious meals without breaking the bank.

4.7 Share Meals or Opt for Small Plates

Consider sharing meals with your travel companions or ordering small plates to sample a variety of dishes without overspending. Many restaurants offer sharing options or tapas-style menus, allowing you to try different flavors while keeping costs in check. Sharing meals not only saves money but also creates a communal dining experience and fosters conversation among fellow travelers.

4.8 Avoid Restaurants in Tourist Hotspots

Restaurants located in popular tourist hotspots often come with inflated prices to cater to tourists. Avoid dining at these establishments and instead explore nearby neighborhoods or side streets where you're more likely to find affordable and authentic dining options. By venturing off the beaten path, you can enjoy local flavors at reasonable prices.

4.9 Research Happy Hour and Drink Specials

If you enjoy an occasional drink, research happy hour and drink specials at local bars and restaurants. Many establishments offer discounted prices during specific hours, allowing you to indulge in your favorite beverages at a more affordable rate. Take advantage of these promotions and enjoy a drink or two without straining your budget

4.10 Bring Your Own Water Bottle and Snacks

To save money on beverages and snacks while exploring, carry a reusable water bottle and pack some snacks. Instead of buying bottled water, refill your water bottle at public fountains or ask for refills at restaurants. This way, you can stay hydrated without constantly purchasing expensive bottled beverages. Similarly, having a few snacks like granola bars, fruit, or nuts on hand can curb hunger pangs and prevent impulsive purchases of overpriced snacks.

4.11 Look for Local Specials and Promotions

Keep an eye out for local specials and promotions that can help you save on dining expenses. Local newspapers, websites, or social media pages often feature restaurant deals, discount coupons, or special offers. Additionally, some cities have designated days or weeks when participating restaurants offer discounted prix-fixe menus or discounts on specific dishes. Stay informed and take advantage of these opportunities to dine out at reduced prices.

4.12 Consider Pre-Theater or Early Bird Menus

If you're planning to attend a theater performance or show, consider dining at restaurants that offer pre-theater or early bird menus. These menus often provide discounted prices for specific dining times, usually before the evening rush. By opting for these menus, you can enjoy a quality meal before your event without paying premium prices. Check with theaters or inquire at nearby restaurants for recommendations.

4.13 Take Advantage of Local Food Apps

In many destinations, there are local food apps or delivery services that offer discounts and promotions for dining out or ordering in. These apps often feature a range of restaurants, allowing you to explore different cuisines and find affordable options. Look for popular local food apps in your destination and check for available deals, discounts, or loyalty programs that can help you save money.

4.14 BYOB (Bring Your Own Bottle) Restaurants

If you enjoy a glass of wine or beer with your meal, consider dining at BYOB restaurants. These establishments allow customers to bring their own alcoholic beverages, often without charging a corkage fee. BYOB restaurants provide an opportunity to enjoy your preferred drinks at retail prices rather than inflated restaurant prices. Check local listings or ask for recommendations to find BYOB restaurants in your destination.

4.15 Take Cooking Classes

Instead of dining out for every meal, consider taking cooking classes to learn how to prepare local dishes. Cooking classes not only provide a fun and educational experience but also allow you to save money by preparing your own meals. You'll learn about local ingredients, cooking techniques, and cultural traditions while enjoying the fruits of your labor. Cooking classes are particularly valuable if you're staying in accommodation with kitchen facilities.

4.16 Consider Buffets or All-You-Can-Eat Options

If you have a hearty appetite or enjoy variety, consider dining at buffets or all-you-can-eat establishments. Buffets often offer a wide selection of dishes for a fixed price, allowing you to sample different cuisines and eat to your heart's content. Make sure to calculate whether the buffet price is reasonable based on the variety and quality of the offerings. Buffets can be a cost-effective option, especially for breakfast or lunch.

4.17 Be Wary of Tourist Traps

Tourist-heavy areas often have restaurants that cater specifically to tourists, offering inflated prices for average or subpar food. Be cautious of these tourist traps and do your research before dining. Look for restaurants frequented by locals or seek recommendations to ensure you find quality meals at fair prices. Checking online reviews and asking for advice from trusted sources can help you avoid disappointments.

4.18 Opt for Takeout or Picnics

In some cases, it may be more budget-friendly to opt for takeout meals or picnics rather than dining in restaurants. Grabbing food from local eateries or street food stalls and enjoying it in a park or scenic spot can be a delightful experience. Takeout meals are often cheaper than eating at a restaurant, and picnics allow you to savor your food while enjoying the ambiance of your surroundings. Pack a blanket and some utensils to make your picnic experience more enjoyable.

4.19 Be Mindful of Tipping Practices

Tipping customs vary from country to country, so be mindful of the tipping practices in your destination. In some places, a service charge may already be included in the bill, while in others, it's customary to leave a gratuity. Understanding local tipping norms can help you budget appropriately and avoid overpaying.

Research the tipping customs or ask locals for guidance to ensure you tip appropriately without overspending.

4.20 Stay Hydrated with Tap Water

In many countries, tap water is safe to drink. Instead of purchasing expensive bottled water at restaurants, request tap water with your meal. It's a cost-effective and eco-friendly option. If you're uncertain about the water quality, carry a portable water filter or purification tablets to ensure you have access to clean drinking water wherever you go.

4.21 Take Advantage of Free Hotel Amenities

If your accommodation offers complimentary breakfast or other meal services, take full advantage of them. Starting your day with a filling breakfast can save you money on your first meal, allowing you to allocate your dining budget more effectively throughout the day. Additionally, some hotels provide free snacks or evening receptions where you can enjoy light refreshments without additional costs.

4.22 Plan Your Splurge Meals

While it's important to stick to your budget, consider planning for a few splurge meals during your trip. Allocate funds for special dining experiences or renowned restaurants that you're particularly interested in. By planning ahead, you can still enjoy memorable culinary experiences without overspending. Prioritize your must-visit restaurants and save money in other areas to accommodate these splurge meals.

4.23 Check for Dining Coupons or Discount Vouchers

Before dining out, check local coupon websites or apps for dining coupons or discount vouchers. These platforms often feature deals for restaurants, allowing you to enjoy discounted meals or special promotions. Keep an eye out for limited-time offers or happy hour discounts that can help you save money while dining out.

4.24 Learn Basic Food Phrases in the Local Language

Learning basic food phrases in the local language can go a long way in saving money and enhancing your dining experience. Being able to communicate your dietary preferences, ask for recommendations, or inquire about vegetarian or vegan options can help you find suitable and affordable meals. Locals appreciate the effort, and you may even receive personalized recommendations or small discounts for trying to speak their language.

4.25 Avoid Ordering Bottled Drinks at Restaurants

Beverages can significantly add to your dining expenses, especially when ordered at restaurants. To save money, consider opting for tap water or other non-alcoholic options. If you prefer alcoholic beverages, choose house wines or local beers, as they are often more affordable compared to premium or imported options. This simple choice can make a noticeable difference in your overall dining bill.

(By implementing these dining and restaurant hacks, you can enjoy delicious meals, experience local flavors, and stick to your budget while traveling. Remember to adapt these tips to suit your specific destination and preferences, and be open to exploring local culinary delights that may surprise and delight you.)

Chapter 5:

Local Transportation

5.1 Research Public Transportation Options

Before arriving at your destination, research the available public transportation options. Familiarize yourself with the local bus, train, tram, or subway systems, as they are often more affordable than taxis or rental cars. Look for information on routes, schedules, and fares to plan your transportation effectively. Public transportation not only saves money but also allows you to experience the local commuting culture.

5.2 Get a Transit Pass or Travel Card

In many cities, purchasing a transit pass or travel card can provide significant savings on transportation costs. These passes often offer unlimited travel within a specified period or provide discounted fares compared to buying individual tickets. Check if your destination offers daily, weekly, or tourist-specific passes and assess whether it aligns with your planned activities. Calculate the potential savings to determine if it's worth investing in a transit pass.

5.3 Walk or Bike Short Distances

When exploring a new city, consider walking or biking for short distances instead of relying on transportation. Not only does it save money, but it also allows you to immerse yourself in the local atmosphere, discover hidden gems, and appreciate the city's architecture and street life. Utilize walking or biking maps, rent bikes if available, and embrace the opportunity to explore your surroundings on foot.

5.4 Use Ride-Sharing Services Wisely

Ride-sharing services like Uber or Lyft can be convenient, but they can also add up in terms of cost. Use ride-sharing services wisely by considering the distance and comparing the price with alternative transportation options. Reserve ride-sharing for situations where it's truly necessary or when traveling with a group, as splitting the fare can make it more affordable. Additionally, keep an eye out for promotions or discount codes to save money on rides.

5.5 Consider Carpooling or Ride-Sharing Apps

If you're traveling with a group or meeting up with other travelers, consider carpooling or using ride-sharing apps specifically designed for sharing rides. These apps connect drivers and passengers heading in the same direction, allowing you to share the cost of transportation. Carpooling not only reduces individual expenses but also minimizes traffic congestion and lowers carbon emissions.

5.6 Negotiate Taxi Fares in Advance

If you need to take a taxi, especially in destinations where meters may not be common, negotiate the fare in advance. Research approximate fares for your route beforehand to have an idea of what's reasonable. Ask locals or your hotel for guidance on customary taxi fares and ensure the driver agrees on the fare before getting in the cab. This practice can help prevent overcharging and unexpected expenses.

5.7 Use Local Ride-Hailing Apps

In addition to global ride-hailing services, many destinations have their own local ride-hailing apps. These apps often offer competitive rates and may have partnerships or deals with local businesses. Research and download popular local ride-hailing apps before your trip to take advantage of any available discounts or promotions. Local apps are also more likely to have drivers who know the city well, ensuring efficient and cost-effective transportation.

5.8 Consider Renting Bicycles or Scooters

If you're comfortable with cycling or riding a scooter, consider renting them as an alternative mode of transportation. Many cities provide bike-sharing programs or scooter rental services that allow you to explore at your own pace. These options are not only eco-friendly but also cost-effective, especially for short-distance travel. Familiarize yourself with local cycling or scooter regulations and safety guidelines before embarking on your two-wheeled adventure.

5.9 Utilize Off-Peak Fares

Public transportation systems often offer off-peak fares during non-peak hours. Take advantage of these discounted fares by planning your travel outside of the busiest times. Not only will you save money, but you'll also experience less crowded trains, buses, or trams, making for a more comfortable journey. Check the local transportation website or inquire at the station for information on off-peak hours and fares.

5.10 Explore Alternative Transportation Methods

In addition to traditional modes of transportation, consider exploring alternative options that may be unique to your destination. For example, some cities have riverboats or ferries that offer scenic routes and can be more affordable than land-based transportation. Cable cars, funiculars, or rickshaws are other interesting options to consider. These alternative methods can provide a memorable experience while saving money on transportation.

5.11 Renting a Car: Compare Prices and Consider Local Agencies

If you decide to rent a car for certain portions of your trip, be sure to compare prices from different rental agencies. Look beyond the well-known international brands and consider local car rental agencies as they may offer competitive rates. However, be mindful of insurance coverage and read the terms and conditions carefully before making a reservation. Depending on your destination and planned activities, renting a car may or may not be the most cost-effective option.

5.12 Use Gas Stations Outside of City Centers

When renting a car, one cost to consider is fuel. To save money on gas, try to fill up your tank at gas stations located outside of city centers. Gas prices are often higher in popular tourist areas, so driving a short distance away from the city center can lead to significant savings. Use navigation apps or ask locals for recommendations on nearby gas stations with more competitive prices.

5.13 Plan Efficient Routes to Minimize Transportation Costs

When sightseeing or exploring multiple attractions in a city, plan your routes efficiently to minimize transportation costs. Group together nearby attractions to avoid unnecessary backtracking or additional transportation expenses. Consider using map apps or public transportation apps to help plan your routes and determine the most cost-effective way to get from one place to another. Being strategic with your itinerary can help you save both time and money.

5.14 Take Advantage of Airport Shuttle Services

If you're arriving at an airport and need transportation to your accommodation, check if there are airport shuttle services available. Many airports offer affordable shuttle buses or vans that can take you directly to popular hotel areas. These services are often cheaper than taking a taxi or private car. Research in advance to find out the schedule, route, and pricing for airport shuttles in your destination.

5.15 Walk or Use Public Transportation in Compact City Centers

In compact city centers with well-connected streets and attractions, walking or using public transportation is often the most convenient and cost-effective option. Instead of relying on taxis or ride-sharing services, explore the city center on foot and utilize the local bus or tram network for longer distances. This way, you can save money while fully experiencing the charm and vibrancy of the city.

(By implementing these travel hacks for local transportation, you can navigate your destination efficiently, save money on transportation expenses, and have a more authentic travel experience. Remember to research your options in advance, plan strategically, and be open to exploring alternative methods of getting around.)

Chapter 6:

Accommodation Hacks

6.1 Compare Prices Across Multiple Platforms

When searching for accommodation, don't limit yourself to a single booking platform. Compare prices across multiple websites, including hotel aggregators, online travel agencies, and the official websites of hotels or guesthouses. Different platforms may offer varying rates, discounts, or promotional offers. Take the time to compare prices and read reviews to find the best value for your desired accommodation.

6.2 Book in Advance for Better Deals

Booking your accommodation in advance can often lead to better deals and discounts. Many hotels offer early bird rates or promotional offers for booking a certain number of days or months ahead. By planning your trip in advance and securing your accommodation early, you can save money and have a wider range of options to choose from. Keep an eye out for any refundable or flexible booking options in case your plans change.

6.3 Consider Alternative Accommodation Options

Explore alternative accommodation options beyond traditional hotels. Consider staying in guesthouses, hostels, vacation rentals, or bed and breakfast establishments. These alternatives can often offer more affordable rates compared to hotels, especially if you're traveling with a group or looking for longer-term stays. Additionally, they may provide a more immersive and unique experience, allowing you to connect with local hosts or fellow travelers.

6.4 Use Incognito Browsing or Clear Browser Cookies

When searching for accommodation online, use incognito browsing or clear your browser cookies. Some booking websites use cookies to track your activity and may increase prices based on your search history. By using incognito mode or clearing cookies, you start each search with a clean slate, potentially avoiding any price hikes that may occur due to your previous searches.

6.5 Sign up for Loyalty Programs

If you frequently travel or plan to stay with a particular hotel chain, sign up for their loyalty program. These programs often provide exclusive benefits such as discounted rates, room upgrades, or complimentary amenities. Accumulating points through loyalty programs can lead to future savings or even free stays. Research

Price Drop Alerts

...tforms or third-party websites offer price
...accommodations. You can set up alerts for
...d if the prices drop, you'll receive
...s you to capitalize on any price reductions
...al. Price drop alerts are particularly useful if
...ip well in advance and have the flexibility to
...gs.

...ong-Term Rentals or Apartment

...r if you prefer more space and privacy,
...entals or apartment shares. Websites and
...to long-term rentals can offer fully furnished
...es at a fraction of the cost of daily hotel rates.
...where you rent a room in someone's home,
...rdable option, especially for solo travelers.
...ad reviews and communicate with the hosts to
...le and safe stay.

...fundable Accommodations for

...s are subject to change or uncertainty, consider
...le accommodations. While refundable rates may
..., they provide the flexibility to cancel or modify
...without incurring significant penalties. This can be
...e unsure about your itinerary or if there's a
...oreseen circumstances affecting your travel plans.
...lation policy carefully to understand any deadlines
...ed with canceling or modifying your booking.

and compare the loyalty programs offered by different hotel chains to find the one that best suits your travel preferences.

6.6 Consider Staying Outside the City Center

Accommodation prices in city centers are often higher due to demand and convenience. Consider staying in neighborhoods or areas just outside the city center where rates may be more affordable. Research the accessibility of public transportation from these locations to ensure that you can easily reach the main attractions. Staying outside the city center can not only save you money but also provide a more local and authentic experience.

6.7 Be Flexible with Your Travel Dates

If your travel dates are flexible, try adjusting them to take advantage of lower accommodation prices. Avoid peak travel seasons or holidays when prices tend to be higher. Instead, consider traveling during shoulder seasons or weekdays when hotels may offer discounted rates to attract guests. Use hotel booking platforms that have flexible date search options to find the most cost-effective periods for your stay.

6.8 Look for Package Deals or Bundled Offers

Some travel websites or booking platforms offer package deals or bundled offers that combine accommodation with other components such as flights or car rentals. These packages can often provide significant savings compared to booking each component separately. If you need multiple travel services, consider bundling them together to take advantage of potential discounts and streamline your planning process.

6.9 Consider Homestays, House-Swapping, or Airbnb

For a unique and cost-effective accommodation experience, consider homestays, house-swapping, or utilizing Airbnb. Homestays involve staying with a local host or family, providing an opportunity to immerse yourself in the local culture and receive insider tips. House-swapping involves exchanging homes with another traveler, allowing you to enjoy the comforts of their home while they stay in yours. Airbnb is a popular online platform that connects travelers with hosts who offer unique accommodations, such as private rooms, apartments, or entire houses.

6.9.1 Homestays:

Homestays can be arranged through dedicated platforms or online communities where locals open their homes to travelers. These accommodations are often more affordable than hotels and provide an opportunity to interact with the host and learn about the local culture. You can find homestays on websites like Homestay.com or through community-driven platforms like Couchsurfing.

6.9.2 House-Swapping:

House-swapping allows you to exchange your home with another traveler, eliminating accommodation costs. Various platforms facilitate house-swapping arrangements, such as HomeExchange, Love Home Swap, or Airbnb's Home Exchange program. House-swapping is an excellent option for longer trips or when you prefer the comfort and amenities of a home.

6.9.3 A

Airbnb has
individuals t
properties to
budget-friend
provide uniqu
allows you to
and guest revi
cost-effective, e

6.10 Negotia

In some cases, es
guesthouses or lo
negotiate for better
seasons or if you're
the property directly
any available discou
accommodations will
can lead to additional

6.11 Stay in All-I

If you're looking for a ha
activities included, consi
hotel. While the upfront c
options can save you mor
to enjoy the on-site ameni
and calculate the potential
paying for activities separat

6.12 Utilize Hotel

Some hotel booking pla
drop alerts for specific
your desired hotels, an
notifications. This allow
and secure a better de
you're planning your tr
wait for potential savin

6.13 Consider L
Shares

For extended stays
consider long-term r
platforms dedicated
apartments or hous
Apartment shares,
can also be an affo
Take the time to re
ensure a comforta

6.14 Book Re
Flexibility

If your travel plan
booking refundab
be slightly higher
your reservation
beneficial if you'
possibility of unf
Read the cance
or fees associa

6.15 Seek Local Recommendations or Stay with Locals

One of the best ways to find affordable and authentic accommodations is by seeking local recommendations or staying with locals. Engage with locals through online travel communities, social media groups, or by reaching out to friends or acquaintances who have connections in your destination. They can provide valuable insights into budget-friendly options, guesthouses, or even spare rooms for rent. Staying with locals not only saves money but also offers an opportunity to connect with the local culture and build meaningful connections.

6.16 Be Mindful of Additional Fees

When booking alternative accommodations, be aware of any additional fees that may apply. Some hosts or platforms may charge cleaning fees, service fees, or security deposits on top of the nightly rate. Take these fees into account when comparing different options to get a more accurate picture of the total cost of your stay. Consider the overall value, including the amenities and services provided, to determine if the accommodation is worth the extra fees.

(By implementing these accommodation hacks, you can find affordable and comfortable places to stay (While traveling. Remember to research and compare prices, be flexible with your dates and location, and consider alternative accommodation options. With a bit of planning and creativity, you can stretch your accommodation budget and have a memorable travel experience.)

Chapter 7:

Transportation Hacks

7.1 Compare Flight Prices on Multiple Platforms

When booking flights, it's essential to compare prices across multiple platforms. Use online travel agencies, airline websites, and flight aggregators to find the best deals. Each platform may have different promotions, discounts, or fare options. Additionally, consider using flexible date search tools to explore alternative travel dates that offer lower fares.

7.2 Be Flexible with Travel Dates and Times

Adaptability with your movement dates and times can prompt critical investment funds. Think about flying on work days or during off-top seasons when passages will quite often be lower. Be open to early morning or late-night flights, as these can often be cheaper than prime-time departures. Use flight search engines that allow you to view prices for a range of dates to find the most cost-effective options.

7.3 Utilize Price Tracking Tools

Take advantage of price tracking tools or fare alerts to monitor flight prices for your desired routes. These tools can alert you when prices drop or when there are special promotions. Set up alerts for specific destinations or travel dates to stay informed and potentially secure better deals. Price tracking tools such as Google Flights, Skyscanner, or Kayak can help you stay updated on price fluctuations.

7.4 Consider Alternative Airports

When searching for flights, consider alternative airports near your origin or destination. Smaller airports or those located in neighboring cities may offer cheaper fares due to lower demand or competition. Compare prices for different airports in the area and consider the cost and convenience of ground transportation to your final destination. Sometimes, the savings from using an alternative airport can outweigh the additional travel time or transportation costs.

7.5 Look for Discount Airlines and Budget Carriers

Discount airlines and budget carriers can offer significantly lower fares compared to full-service airlines. Research and compare different airlines, including regional or low-cost carriers, to find the most affordable options. Be aware of any additional fees for baggage, seat selection, or in-flight services, as these may vary between airlines. However, even with the extra fees, budget airlines can still provide substantial savings.

7.6 Consider Connecting Flights

Direct flights are commonly more convenient, but they can also be more expensive. If you're willing to spend a little more time traveling, consider booking connecting flights instead. Connecting flights can sometimes result in lower fares, especially if you're flexible with layover durations. However, be mindful of the layover times to ensure you have enough time to make your connecting flight without rushing.

7.7 Book in Advance, but not Too Far in Advance

While booking in advance can secure better fares, it's essential to find the right balance. Airlines often release their flight schedules and tickets around 6 to 9 months in advance. Booking too far ahead may limit your flexibility and options, as airlines may not have released their most competitive fares yet. On the other hand, last-minute bookings can be expensive. Aim to book your flights about 3 to 4 months before your travel date for the best combination of price and availability.

7.8 Use Frequent Flyer Programs and Travel Rewards Credit Cards

If you're a frequent traveler, consider joining frequent flyer programs offered by airlines. Accumulating miles or points through these programs can lead to free flights, upgrades, or other travel-related benefits. Additionally, consider using travel rewards credit cards that allow you to earn points or miles for your everyday purchases. These points can be redeemed for flights, hotel stays, or other travel expenses, helping you save money on your overall travel costs.

7.9 Explore Alternative Modes of Transportation

Depending on your destination and travel preferences, consider exploring alternative modes of transportation besides flying. Train travel, bus services, or even carpooling can be cost-effective options, especially for shorter distances or regional travel. Research the availability and cost of train or bus tickets and compare them to flight prices. In some cases, taking a scenic train journey or a comfortable bus ride can be a more affordable and enjoyable option, allowing you to experience the landscape and local culture along the way.

7.10 Use Ride-Sharing and Car Rental Comparison Apps

When it comes to ground transportation, ride-sharing services like Uber or Lyft can be convenient and cost-effective, especially for short distances or when traveling in groups. Use ride-sharing comparison apps to compare prices and availability across different services. Additionally, if you plan to rent a car, utilize car rental comparison platforms to find the best deals. Compare prices, vehicle options, and rental terms from multiple rental companies to secure the most affordable and suitable car rental for your needs.

7.11 Consider Public Transportation

Utilizing public transportation in your destination city can be a great way to save money while getting around. Research the availability of buses, trams, subways, or trains, and familiarize yourself with their routes and ticketing options. Many cities offer discounted multi-day or unlimited travel passes, which can provide significant savings if you plan to use public transportation frequently.

7.12 Walk or Bike When Possible

Exploring your destination on foot or by bike not only saves money but also allows you to immerse yourself in the local environment. Many cities have well-developed pedestrian and cycling infrastructure, making it easy and enjoyable to navigate on foot or by bicycle. Walking or cycling between nearby attractions or neighborhoods can save transportation costs while providing a more intimate and unique experience.

7.13 Research Local Transportation Apps and Passes

Before arriving at your destination, research and download any local transportation apps that may provide information on routes, schedules, and real-time updates. These apps can be particularly useful for navigating public transportation systems efficiently. Additionally, check if there are discounted or bundled transportation passes available for tourists, allowing unlimited travel on buses, trams, or subways for a specified duration.

7.14 Pack Light to Avoid Excess Baggage Fees

Many airlines charge additional fees for checked baggage, especially on budget carriers. To avoid these fees, pack light and prioritize essential items. Check the baggage allowance and restrictions for your specific airline, and consider using a carry-on bag or opting for airlines with more generous baggage policies. Packing efficiently can save you money and provide the flexibility to travel hassle-free with just your carry-on.

7.15 Consider Car-Sharing or Carpooling Services

If you're traveling with a group or planning to explore areas beyond the reach of public transportation, consider car-sharing or carpooling services. Platforms like Turo or Zipcar allow you to rent cars from local owners, often at lower rates than traditional car rental companies. Carpooling services like Uber and Lyft connect drivers with passengers traveling in the same direction, enabling cost-sharing and reducing individual transportation expenses.

7.16 Research Local Parking Options and Costs

If you plan to rent a car or drive in your destination, research local parking options and costs in advance. Some cities offer affordable or even free parking areas, while others have expensive parking rates, especially in city centers. Look for public parking garages, parking apps, or street parking regulations to find the most cost-effective and convenient options for parking your vehicle.

7.17 Be Mindful of Toll Roads and Road Fees

If you're embarking on a road trip, be aware of toll roads, vignettes, or road fees that may apply in certain regions or countries. Research the specific routes you'll be traveling and the associated fees to include them in your budget. In some cases, alternative routes or pre-purchasing electronic toll tags or vignettes can help reduce the overall cost of your journey.

(By applying these transportation hacks, including comparing flight prices on multiple platforms, being flexible with travel dates and times, utilizing price tracking tools, considering alternative airports, and exploring budget airlines, you can find affordable air travel options. Additionally, by using ride-sharing services, comparing car rental options, considering public transportation, walking or biking when possible, and researching local transportation apps and passes, you can save money on ground transportation expenses. Remember to pack light to avoid excess baggage fees, explore car-sharing or carpooling services, research local parking options and costs, and be mindful of toll roads and road fees to further optimize your transportation expenses.)

Chapter 8:

Dining and Food Hacks

8.1 Explore Local Food Markets and Street Vendors

One of the best ways to experience the local cuisine and save money on dining is by exploring food markets and street vendors. These places offer a wide variety of affordable and authentic dishes, allowing you to taste local specialties without breaking the bank. Interact with the vendors, ask for recommendations, and indulge in the vibrant flavors of the local street food scene.

8.2 Research Affordable Eateries in Advance

Before you arrive at your destination, research affordable eateries in the area. Use travel websites, review platforms, and local food blogs to find budget-friendly restaurants and cafes that offer good value for money. Look for places that locals frequent, as they often provide authentic dining experiences at reasonable prices.

8.3 Take Advantage of Lunch Specials and Set Menus

Many restaurants offer lunch specials or set menus during certain hours of the day. These options
often provide a more affordable way to enjoy a complete meal compared to ordering à la carte. Take advantage of these offers and plan your sightseeing or activities around these lunchtime deals to enjoy delicious meals at a discounted price.

8.4 Opt for Local Neighborhoods Instead of Tourist Areas

Restaurants located in touristy areas tend to be more expensive. To save money on dining, venture into local neighborhoods where the prices are typically lower. Explore local restaurants, cafes, and eateries frequented by residents to get a taste of authentic cuisine at a more affordable price point.

8.5 Cook Your Own Meals

If you have access to a kitchen or are staying in accommodations with cooking facilities, consider preparing some of your meals. Visit local markets or grocery stores to purchase fresh ingredients and cook simple meals that reflect the local cuisine. Not only will this save you money, but it can also be a fun and rewarding culinary experience.

8.6 Pack Snacks and Picnic Supplies

To avoid expensive snacks or meals on the go, pack your own snacks and picnic supplies. Carry a reusable water bottle, granola bars, fruits, and other non-perishable snacks to keep you fueled throughout the day. Additionally, pick up some local bread, cheese, and deli items to create your own picnic lunch while enjoying scenic spots or parks.

8.7 Happy Hours and Drink Specials

If you enjoy a drink or two during your travels, take advantage of happy hours and drink specials offered by bars and restaurants. These promotions often provide discounted prices on beverages, allowing you to enjoy a refreshing drink without breaking your budget. Research local establishments and their happy hour timings to make the most of these deals.

8.8 Share Meals or Order Small Plates

When dining out, consider sharing meals with your travel companions or ordering small plates to sample a variety of dishes. Many restaurants offer generous portion sizes, and sharing can help reduce costs while allowing you to savor different flavors. This approach is particularly beneficial In places with tapas-style dining or where family-style meals are common.

8.9 Seek Out Local Food Events and Festivals

Check if there are any local food events or festivals taking place during your visit. These events often feature affordable food stalls, showcasing the region's culinary delights. It's an excellent opportunity to try a variety of dishes at reasonable prices while immersing yourself in the vibrant atmosphere of the event.

8.10 Ask Locals for Dining Recommendations

Locals are often the best source of information when it comes to finding hidden gems and affordable dining options. Strike up conversations with locals, hotel staff, or taxi drivers, and ask for their recommendations for authentic yet budget-friendly eateries. They can provide valuable insights and steer you towards local favorites that may not be as well-known to tourists.

8.11 Take Advantage of Restaurant Discounts and Coupons

Before arriving at your destination, search for restaurant discounts and coupons available online or through local tourist guides. Many cities have websites or apps that offer deals and discounts for various restaurants. Look for promotional codes, printable coupons, or digital vouchers that can help you save money on your dining expenses. Make sure to read the terms and conditions of the discounts to ensure they are applicable during your visit.

8.12 Dine during Off-Peak Hours

Consider dining during off-peak hours, such as early dinner or late lunch, as some restaurants offer discounted prices during these times. By avoiding the rush hour, you may have a better chance of securing a table without a reservation and enjoy lower prices or special promotions.

8.13 Look for All-Inclusive Meal Deals

In popular tourist destinations, some restaurants offer all-inclusive meal deals that include multiple courses, beverages, and even entertainment. These deals can provide excellent value for money, especially if you're planning to indulge in a more elaborate dining experience. Compare prices and offerings to find the best all-inclusive deals that suit your preferences.

8.14 Take Advantage of Loyalty Programs

If you frequently visit a particular restaurant chain or coffee shop, consider signing up for their loyalty programs. These programs often offer rewards, discounts, or freebies based on your purchases. Accumulate points or stamps with each visit and redeem them for discounted or free meals in the future.

8.15 Avoid Tourist Trap Restaurants

Tourist trap restaurants located near popular attractions tend to charge higher prices while offering mediocre quality. Avoid falling into these traps by researching reviews and recommendations from trusted sources. Look for local establishments that prioritize quality and authenticity, even if they are situated slightly away from the main tourist areas.

8.16 Learn Basic Food Phrases and Etiquette

Learning a few basic food phrases and understanding local dining etiquette can go a long way in enhancing your dining experience. It shows respect for the local culture and can help you communicate your preferences or dietary restrictions effectively. Knowing how to say "please," "thank you," or asking for recommendations in the local language can create a positive impression and potentially lead to better service.

8.17 Embrace Cultural Differences in Dining Customs

Each destination has its own dining customs and practices. Embrace these cultural differences and adapt to the local customs when dining out. For example, in some countries, it's customary to share dishes, while in others, it's considered polite to finish everything you have on your plate. Respecting and embracing these customs not only enhances your cultural experience but also allows you to fully immerse yourself in the local dining scene.

8.18 Use Review Platforms and Social Media for Recommendations

Harness the power of review platforms and social media to find reliable recommendations for dining options. Platforms like TripAdvisor, Yelp, and local food blogs provide insights from fellow travelers and locals. Read reviews, browse through photos, and take note of highly-rated establishments that offer excellent value for money.

(By implementing these dining and food hacks, including exploring local food markets and street vendors, researching affordable eateries, cooking your own meals, and seeking out local recommendations, you can enjoy delicious meals while keeping your dining expenses under control. Remember to balance your desire to try local cuisine with cost-effective choices to make the most of your culinary experiences while staying within your travel budget.)

Chapter 9:

Local Experiences and Activities Hacks

9.1 Research Free or Low-Cost Attractions

Before your trip, research the destination's free or low-cost attractions. Many cities have parks, museums with free admission days, public art installations, or historic sites that can be explored without breaking the bank. By planning your itinerary around these budget-friendly attractions, you can have a fulfilling travel experience without spending a fortune.

9.2 Take Advantage of City Tourism Cards

Many cities offer tourism cards or passes that provide discounts or free entry to popular attractions, museums, and public transportation. These cards are often available for a fixed duration, such as 24 hours or 72 hours, and can help you save money while exploring multiple sites. Compare the available options and calculate the potential savings to determine if purchasing a tourism card is beneficial for your travel plans.

9.3 Look for Local Festivals and Events

Check if there are any local festivals, cultural events, or celebrations happening during your visit. These events often showcase the region's traditions, music, dance, and cuisine. Participating in these festivities can provide unique and memorable experiences without a hefty price tag. Keep an eye out for community events, street parades, or outdoor concerts that are free or have a nominal entrance fee.

9.4 Explore Nature and Outdoor Activities

Nature provides abundant opportunities for exploration and adventure at little to no cost. Research local hiking trails, parks, beaches, or scenic viewpoints where you can immerse yourself in the natural beauty of your destination. Whether it's hiking, swimming, cycling, or simply enjoying a picnic in the park, outdoor activities can be an affordable and rejuvenating way to experience the local surroundings.

9.5 Seek Out Local Experiences

Engaging in local experiences is a great way to delve into the culture and traditions of a place while supporting the local community. Look for workshops, cooking classes, handicraft demonstrations, or cultural performances offered by local artisans, organizations, or community centers. These activities often provide hands-on experiences and insights into the local way of life at a reasonable cost.

9.6 Take Walking Tours

Walking tours led by knowledgeable local guides can be an excellent way to explore a city's highlights while learning about its history and culture. Many cities offer free walking tours where you can join a group and explore various attractions on foot. Alternatively, you can opt for affordable paid walking tours that focus on specific themes or neighborhoods. Walking tours provide an interactive and educational experience while being easy on the wallet.

9.7 Volunteer or Work Exchange Programs

Consider participating in volunteer programs or work exchange opportunities during your travels. These programs allow you to contribute your skills and time in exchange for accommodation, meals, or a stipend. Engaging in volunteer work not only provides a chance to give back to the local community but also offers a unique perspective and deeper immersion into the destination's culture.

9.8 Utilize Local Transportation for Sightseeing

Instead of opting for expensive tourist buses or guided tours, use the local public transportation system for sightseeing. Research bus routes, tram lines, or subway networks that pass by major landmarks and attractions. This not only saves money but also allows you to experience the city like a local, observing everyday life and getting a more authentic feel for the destination.

9.9 Attend Free Cultural Performances and Exhibitions

Many cities host free cultural performances, concerts, or art exhibitions throughout the year. Check local event listings, community bulletin boards, or tourist information centers to find out about upcoming events. Whether it's a street performance, live music in a park, or an art gallery showcasing local talent, these events offer entertainment and cultural experiences without any cost.

9.10 Connect with Local Communities through Social Networks

Use social networks and online platforms to connect with locals or expats residing in your destination. Websites like Meetup, Couchsurfing, or local Facebook groups can help you find like-minded individuals or community events happening during your visit. Engaging with locals can lead to authentic experiences, insider tips, and the opportunity to participate in local gatherings or activities that may not be widely advertised.

9.11 Take Advantage of Free Guided Tours

Some attractions, such as museums, historical sites, or cultural institutions, offer free guided tours at specific times or days. Take advantage of these opportunities to gain deeper insights into the exhibits or locations while benefiting from the expertise of knowledgeable guides. Check the attraction's website or inquire at the information desk for details on free guided tours.

9.12 Visit Local Libraries and Cultural Centers

Local libraries and cultural centers often host events, lectures, or workshops that are open to the public. These venues can provide valuable resources, information, and opportunities to engage with the local community. Attend book readings, art exhibitions, or cultural talks to expand your knowledge and connect with people who share similar interests.

9.13 Explore Neighborhoods Off the Beaten Path

While popular tourist areas may have their charm, exploring neighborhoods off the beaten path can offer unique and authentic experiences. Wander through residential areas, visit local markets, or seek out hidden gems recommended by locals. This allows you to discover the true essence of a place, interact with friendly residents, and stumble upon affordable dining options or quaint shops.

9.14 Participate in Free or Discounted Outdoor Activities

Many destinations offer free or discounted outdoor activities, such as yoga in the park, group exercise classes, or guided hikes. Research if there are any community programs or recreational organizations that provide such opportunities. Participating in these activities not only allows you to stay active and enjoy the outdoors but also gives you a chance to meet fellow travelers and locals.

9.15 Take Advantage of Student Discounts

If you're a student, remember to carry your student ID card with you. Many attractions, museums, theaters, and transportation services offer discounted rates for students. Take advantage of these discounts by presenting your valid student ID and save money on various activities and services during your travels.

9.16 Attend Local Sporting Events or Games

If there's a local sports team in the city you're visiting, attending a sporting event or game can be a thrilling and budget-friendly experience. Check the local sports schedule and purchase tickets for matches or games. Whether it's soccer, basketball, cricket, or any other sport, cheering for the home team alongside enthusiastic locals can create memorable moments.

9.17 Utilize Online Coupon Platforms and Discount Websites

Explore online coupon platforms and discount websites specific to your destination. These platforms offer deals and discounts on various activities, attractions, and experiences. Look for discounted tickets, package deals, or promotional codes that can significantly reduce the cost of popular tourist activities or adventure outings.

9.18 Be Open to Spontaneous Opportunities

Lastly, be open to spontaneous opportunities that may arise during your travels. Keep an eye out for flyers, posters, or notices about local events, workshops, or performances. Sometimes, the most memorable experiences come from stumbling upon something unexpected and embracing the moment.

(By incorporating these local experiences and activities into your travel plans, you can immerse yourself in the culture, engage with

the local community, and enjoy unique experiences without straining your budget. Remember to prioritize meaningful connections, explore off-the-beaten-path locations, and take advantage of the diverse range of free or affordable activities available at your destination.)

Chapter 10:

Safety and Security Hacks

10.1 Research Travel Advisories and Safety Precautions

Before embarking on your journey, research travel advisories and safety precautions specific to your destination. Check the official websites of your country's foreign affairs department or government travel advisories for up-to-date information on potential risks, safety guidelines, and any necessary precautions to take while traveling. Stay informed about the current situation and follow the recommended safety measures.

10.2 Secure Your Belongings

Keep your belongings secure to minimize the risk of theft or loss. Invest in a reliable travel lock or combination lock to secure your luggage. Use hotel safes or secure lockers for storing valuable items when you're out exploring. Consider using a money belt or hidden pouch to carry important documents, cash, and cards discreetly. Be mindful of your surroundings and avoid displaying expensive items that may attract unwanted attention.

10.3 Use a VPN and Secure Wi-Fi Connections

Protect your digital privacy and sensitive information by using a virtual private network (VPN) when accessing public Wi-Fi networks. A VPN encrypts your internet connection and ensures your data remains secure from potential hackers. Furthermore, be wary while interfacing with public Wi-Fi organizations and abstain from getting to delicate data or making monetary exchanges except if you're utilizing a protected association.

10.4 Share Itinerary and Emergency Contacts

Share your travel itinerary, including accommodation details, transportation arrangements, and contact information, with a trusted friend or family member. In case of an emergency or unforeseen situation, they will have a clear understanding of your whereabouts and can provide assistance if needed. Carry a copy of important emergency contacts, including local authorities and embassy/consulate information, in case of emergencies.

10.5 Stay Vigilant in Crowded Areas

When traveling to crowded areas, such as markets, tourist attractions, or public transportation hubs, be aware of your surroundings and keep a close eye on your belongings. Pickpockets often operate in crowded places, so ensure your bags are securely closed and avoid displaying valuable items. Stay vigilant and trust your instincts if something feels suspicious or uncomfortable.

10.6 Familiarize Yourself with Local Laws and Customs

Research and familiarize yourself with the local laws, customs, and cultural norms of your destination. Respect local customs, dress modestly when required, and adhere to any specific guidelines or restrictions. Understanding and abiding by local laws not only ensures your safety but also shows respect for the local culture.

10.7 Carry Emergency Cash and Backup Documents

Carry a sufficient amount of emergency cash in a separate location from your main wallet or purse. This can be helpful in case of theft, loss, or unexpected situations where card payments may not be accepted. Additionally, carry backup copies of important travel documents, such as your passport, identification cards, and travel insurance information. Store these copies in a secure location, separate from the originals.

10.8 Be Mindful of Scams and Tourist Traps

Be cautious of common travel scams and tourist traps that target unsuspecting tourists. Research common scams in your destination and stay informed about the latest tactics used by scammers. Be skeptical of overly friendly strangers offering unsolicited help or too-good-to-be-true deals. Use official taxi services, verify prices before entering into agreements, and exercise caution when sharing personal or financial information.

10.9 Register with Your Embassy or Consulate

Register with your embassy or consulate before your trip or upon arrival at your destination. This allows your government to assist you in case of emergencies, natural disasters, or other critical situations. Provide them with your contact information and travel details, and stay updated with any travel advisories or alerts issued by your embassy or consulate.

10.10 Purchase Travel Insurance

Invest in comprehensive travel insurance that covers medical expenses, trip cancellation or interruption of flights and protects you against risk and financial loss that can happen while traveling.

10.10.1 Evaluate Your Coverage Needs

When purchasing travel insurance, carefully evaluate your coverage needs based on the type of trip you're taking, your destination, and any specific activities or risks involved. Ensure that your policy covers medical emergencies, trip cancellation or interruption, lost or delayed baggage, emergency evacuation, and personal liability.

10.10.2 Compare Policies and Providers

Research different travel insurance providers and compare their policies to find the best coverage at a competitive price. Read the policy terms and conditions carefully, including the coverage limits, exclusions, and any additional options or add-ons available. Look for reputable insurance companies with a reliable claims process and positive customer reviews.

10.10.3 Understand Policy Exclusions and Limitations

Be aware of the exclusions and limitations of your travel insurance policy. Certain activities, pre-existing medical conditions, or high-risk destinations may not be covered. Read the fine print and ask questions to ensure you have a clear understanding of what is and isn't covered by your policy. Consider purchasing additional coverage or specialized policies if needed.

10.10.4 Keep Copies of Insurance Documents Handy

Make copies of your travel insurance policy documents, including contact numbers, claim procedures, and emergency assistance details. Keep one copy with you and leave another copy with a trusted person back home. Additionally, consider storing digital copies of your insurance documents on your smartphone or cloud storage for easy access during your trip.

10.10.5 Familiarize Yourself with the Claims Process

Before your trip, familiarize yourself with the claims process of your travel insurance provider. Understand the steps to follow in case of an emergency or if you need to file a claim. Keep all relevant receipts, medical reports, or documentation required for claim submission. Contact your insurance provider promptly in case of any emergency or covered event.

(By implementing these safety and security hacks, you can enhance your personal safety, protect your belongings, and mitigate potential risks during your travels. Prioritize your well-being, stay informed, and take necessary precautions to ensure a safe and secure journey. Remember that being prepared and proactive is key to enjoying a worry-free travel experience.)

Bonus Travel Hacks

Chapter 11:

Traveling with Children Hacks

11.1 Packing Essentials for Traveling with Children

Provide a checklist of essential items to pack when traveling with children, including diapers, wipes, extra clothes, snacks, entertainment items (books, toys, games), and comfort items (blankets, stuffed animals).

Offer tips on organizing and packing these items efficiently to maximize space and accessibility during the trip.

Suggest travel-friendly gear such as lightweight strollers, baby carriers, or portable high chairs that can make navigating airports and attractions easier.

11.2 Entertainment Options for Children during Travel

Share a variety of entertainment ideas to keep children engaged during long flights, car rides, or train journeys.

Recommend portable electronic devices loaded with child-friendly apps, movies, or games.

Provide suggestions for travel-friendly activities like coloring books, sticker books, travel-sized board games, or interactive toys.

11.3 Managing Jet Lag for Children

Offer strategies for minimizing the effects of jet lag on children, such as adjusting sleep schedules a few days before the trip, encouraging natural light exposure at the destination, and maintaining consistent meal times.

Provide tips for helping children sleep better during flights or in new environments, including bringing familiar bedding or comfort items, creating a soothing bedtime routine, and using white noise machines or relaxation techniques.

11.4 Child-Friendly Attractions and Activities

Recommend child-friendly attractions and activities at various destinations, highlighting interactive museums, theme parks, zoos, or nature parks that cater to children's interests.

Suggest family-friendly tours or experiences, such as boat rides, nature walks, or kid-friendly cooking classes, that can be enjoyable for both parents and children.

11.5 Choosing Family-Friendly Accommodations

Advise on selecting accommodations that cater to families, including options with family rooms, extra beds, or child-friendly amenities like play areas, swimming pools, or childcare services.

Provide tips for booking accommodations in convenient locations near attractions or public transportation for easier logistics.

11.6 Dining Tips for Traveling with Children

Offer advice on finding child-friendly restaurants or cafes that provide kid's menus, high chairs, or play areas.

Suggest ways to navigate picky eaters or dietary restrictions by carrying familiar snacks, exploring local markets for fresh fruits or snacks, or involving children in meal planning or food exploration.

11.7 Safety Considerations for Traveling with Children

Provide safety tips for traveling with children, including staying vigilant in crowded areas, keeping an eye on children near bodies of water or high-traffic areas, and carrying identification or emergency contact information.

Advise on using child safety devices such as child proofing kits, outlet covers, or portable safety gates to ensure a safe environment in accommodations.

11.8 Traveling with Infants or Toddlers

Offer specific tips for traveling with infants or toddlers, including packing essentials like baby carriers, nursing covers, or portable changing mats.

Provide guidance on managing nap times and feeding schedules during travel, including recommendations for breastfeeding mothers or formula-feeding parents.

11.9 Navigating Airports and Security Procedures

Share tips for navigating airports and security procedures with children, including advice on packing snacks or drinks for the journey, carrying necessary documents, and using family-friendly security lanes or priority boarding options.

11.10 Embracing the Family Travel Experience

Encourage parents to embrace the joys and challenges of family travel, emphasizing the importance of flexibility, patience, and creating lasting memories

.

Share inspiring stories or experiences from other families who have traveled with children to motivate and reassure parents.

(By including these tips and hacks for traveling with children, the book provides valuable insights and practical advice for families embarking on adventures together. It aims to make the travel experience enjoyable.)

Chapter 12:

<u>Sustainable Travel Hacks</u>

12.1 Pack Light and Thoughtfully

Encourage travelers to pack light to reduce carbon emissions associated with transportation.
Suggest using sustainable travel gear like reusable water bottles, eco-friendly toiletries, and lightweight, durable luggage made from sustainable materials.
Emphasize the importance of packing only what is necessary to minimize waste and conserve resources.

12.2 Choose Eco-Friendly Accommodations

Provide tips for selecting eco-friendly accommodations, such as hotels with green certifications or eco-lodges that prioritize sustainable practices
.
Highlight eco-conscious features like energy-efficient lighting, water-saving initiatives, and waste reduction programs.
Recommend researching and supporting accommodations that actively contribute to local environmental conservation efforts.

12.3 Support Local and Sustainable Tourism Initiatives

Encourage travelers to support local businesses, artisans, and farmers by purchasing locally made products and souvenirs.

.

Promote sustainable tourism initiatives like community-based tourism or responsible wildlife tourism that prioritize conservation and benefit local communities.

Suggest seeking out eco-friendly tour operators and guides who prioritize responsible practices and environmental education.

12.4 Reduce Plastic Usage

Offer tips for minimizing plastic waste during travel, such as carrying a reusable shopping bag, reusable utensils, and a stainless-steel straw.

Encourage travelers to refill water bottles from filtered water stations or carry water purification devices to avoid purchasing single-use plastic water bottles.

Recommend choosing restaurants and cafes that use biodegradable or compostable packaging.

12.5 Conserve Water and Energy

Provide suggestions for conserving water and energy in accommodations, such as taking shorter showers, reusing towels, and turning off lights and air conditioning when leaving the room.

Encourage travelers to participate in programs that reward guests for conserving resources, such as towel reuse programs or energy-saving initiatives.

12.6 Use Sustainable Transportation

Promote eco-friendly transportation options, such as walking, cycling, or using public transportation when exploring destinations.

Encourage travelers to offset their carbon footprint by supporting carbon offset projects or opting for carbon-neutral transportation alternatives like electric or hybrid vehicles.

12.7 Respect Local Cultures and Environments

Emphasize the importance of respecting local cultures, customs, and traditions when visiting different destinations.
Encourage travelers to learn about and follow local environmental guidelines, such as respecting protected areas, wildlife habitats, and marine ecosystems.

Advocate for responsible behavior, such as not littering, avoiding excessive noise, and refraining from touching or disturbing wildlife.

12.8 Participate In Volunteering or Conservation Activities

Encourage travelers to engage in volunteer work or conservation activities that contribute positively to local communities and environments.

Provide resources for finding volunteer opportunities related to environmental conservation, community development, or wildlife protection.

12.9 Educate and Raise Awareness

Highlight the importance of spreading awareness about sustainable travel practices among friends, family, and fellow travelers.

Encourage travelers to share their experiences and insights on social media, blogs, or travel forums to inspire others to adopt sustainable travel habits.

12.10 Leave a Positive Impact

Reinforce the idea that sustainable travel is about leaving a positive impact on the destinations visited.

Encourage travelers to leave places cleaner than they found them, support local initiatives, and engage in responsible tourism practices that contribute to the long-term well-being of local communities and environments.

(By incorporating these sustainable travel hacks, the book empowers travelers to make conscious choices that reduce their environmental impact, preserve natural resources, and support local communities, ultimately creating a more sustainable and responsible travel experience.)

Chapter 13:

<u>Solo Travel Hacks</u>

13.1 Embrace Your Independence

Encourage solo travelers to embrace the freedom and flexibility that comes with traveling alone.
Highlight the opportunities for self-discovery, personal growth, and building confidence that solo travel can provide.

13.2 Plan and Research

Provide tips for solo travelers to thoroughly research their destination, including understanding local customs, cultural norms, and safety considerations.

Recommend creating a detailed itinerary and sharing it with trusted family or friends for added safety.

13.3 Safety and Security

Offer practical advice for solo travelers to prioritize personal safety, such as staying aware of their surroundings, avoiding risky areas or situations, and trusting their instincts.
Suggest carrying a personal safety alarm, keeping emergency contact numbers handy, and notifying someone of their daily whereabouts.

13.4 Connect with Other Travelers

Encourage solo travelers to seek opportunities to connect with fellow travelers, such as staying in social accommodations like hostels or participating in group activities or tours.

Recommend using online travel communities, forums, or social media groups to connect with like-minded individuals or find travel companions.

13.5 Solo-Friendly Accommodations

Provide tips for finding solo-friendly accommodations, including hostels with private rooms, guesthouses, or small boutique hotels that offer a social atmosphere and opportunities to meet other travelers.

Suggest using reputable accommodation booking platforms and reading reviews from other solo travelers.

13.6 Dining Alone with Confidence

Offer strategies for dining alone with confidence, such as choosing busy restaurants or cafes, bringing a book or journal, or utilizing smartphone apps that connect solo diners with communal tables or dining groups.

Encourage solo travelers to embrace the experience of trying local cuisine and exploring new dining venues.

13.7 Exploring with Caution

Advise solo travelers to explore during daylight hours and inform someone of their planned activities for the day.

Recommend using reliable transportation options and being cautious when accepting invitations or assistance from strangers.

13.8 Trusting Local Recommendations

Encourage solo travelers to seek recommendations from locals, such as hotel staff, tour guides, or fellow travelers, for authentic experiences and hidden gems.

Highlight the value of connecting with locals to gain insights into the culture, traditions, and off-the-beaten-path attractions.

13.9 Documenting the Journey

Suggest creative ways for solo travelers to document their journey, such as keeping a travel journal, capturing photographs, or starting a blog or vlog to share their experiences.

Emphasize the importance of capturing memories while still being present in the moment.

13.10 Self-Care and Reflection

Stress the significance of self-care during solo travel, including taking breaks, practicing mindfulness, and staying connected with loved ones. Encourage solo travelers to reflect on their experiences, set personal goals, and embrace the transformative nature of solo travel.

(By including these solo travel hacks, the book aims to empower individuals to embark on solo adventures with confidence, offering practical advice to ensure a safe, enriching, and memorable journey.)

Chapter 14:

Traveling on a Budget Hacks (Advanced)

14.1 Mastering Flight Deals

Provide advanced strategies for finding the best flight deals, including utilizing travel rewards programs, credit card points, and airline alliances.
Recommend booking open-jaw or multi-city itineraries to save on airfare and explore multiple destinations in one trip. Offer tips for using flight search engines effectively, such as flexible date searches, setting fare alerts, and booking during off-peak times.

14.2 Accommodation Savings

Share advanced techniques for maximizing accommodation savings, such as utilizing house-sitting opportunities, home exchanges, or vacation rentals through platforms like Airbnb or HomeAway.

Encourage travelers to consider last-minute deals or off-season stays for discounted rates.
Highlight the benefits of alternative accommodations like hostels, guesthouses, or budget hotels for budget-conscious travelers.

14.3 Dining on a Budget

Provide tips for saving money on meals while traveling, such as exploring local markets and street food stalls for affordable and authentic dining experiences.

Recommend trying local cuisine at inexpensive eateries and avoiding touristy restaurants that often come with higher prices.

Suggest booking accommodations with kitchen facilities to prepare some meals or snacks and reduce dining expenses.

14.4 Transportation Savings

Offer strategies for saving money on transportation, such as using public transportation instead of taxis or rental cars.

Encourage travelers to explore walking or cycling as a means of transportation within cities.
Highlight the benefits of using ride-sharing services or shared shuttle services for airport transfers.

14.5 Free and Discounted Activities

Provide a list of free or discounted activities and attractions at popular destinations, such as free museum days, walking tours, or local festivals.
Suggest checking for city tourism cards or passes that offer discounted or bundled access to multiple attractions.

Encourage travelers to seek out local deals and discounts through websites, apps, or travel guides.

14.6 Budget-Friendly Shopping

Offer tips for shopping on a budget while traveling, such as visiting local markets or flea markets for unique and affordable souvenirs.

Recommend bargaining or negotiating prices at street markets where it is culturally acceptable.
Encourage travelers to compare prices at different stores or stalls before making a purchase.

14.7 Currency Exchange and Transaction Fees

Provide advice on avoiding unnecessary currency exchange fees by using ATMs or credit cards with low foreign transaction fees.

Suggest researching local banks or exchange offices that offer competitive exchange rates.
Recommend carrying a mix of cash and cards for convenience and backup.

14.8 Budget-Friendly Destinations

Share a list of budget-friendly destinations that offer affordable accommodations, food, and attractions.
Highlight lesser-known destinations or off-the-beaten-path locations that offer unique experiences at a lower cost.

Provide tips for finding budget-friendly destinations during specific times of the year, such as shoulder seasons or offseason travel.

14.9 Travel Insurance and Health Savings

Emphasize the importance of travel insurance to protect against unexpected expenses, such as medical emergencies or trip cancellations.
Recommend comparing different insurance providers to find the most affordable and comprehensive coverage.

Advise travelers to carry a basic travel medical kit to handle minor health issues and avoid overpriced medications while abroad.

14.10 Embracing the Thrifty Traveler Lifestyle

Encourage travelers to embrace the thrifty traveler lifestyle by focusing on experiences rather than material possessions.

Share stories and tips from experienced budget travelers who have mastered the art of exploring the world on a limited budget.

Inspire readers to find joy in the simplicity of budget travel and the unique opportunities it offers.

(By including these advanced budget travel hacks, the book provides readers with the tools and knowledge to plan and execute cost-effective travel experiences without sacrificing quality or enjoyment)

Chapter 15:

<u>Traveling with Kids Hacks Advanced</u>

15.1 Plan Kid-Friendly Activities

Provide tips for researching and planning kid-friendly activities and attractions at the destination.

Recommend visiting parks, zoos, interactive museums, or family-friendly festivals.
Suggest checking online resources or travel guides specifically designed for family travel.

15.2 Pack Wisely for Kids

Offer suggestions for packing essentials for traveling with kids, including extra clothing, diapers, wipes, and snacks.

Provide tips for organizing and packing children's items efficiently, such as using packing cubes or separate bags for each child.
Encourage travelers to carry comfort items like favorite toys or blankets to help children feel secure.

15.3 Choose Family-Friendly Accommodations

Highlight the importance of selecting family-friendly accommodations that offer amenities like cribs, high chairs, or play areas.

Suggest booking accommodations with kitchen facilities to prepare meals and accommodate children's dietary needs.

Encourage researching accommodations with kid-friendly activities or childcare services.

15.4 Plan for Child-Friendly Transportation

Provide tips for navigating transportation with children, such as booking direct flights or considering shorter travel durations.

Recommend bringing entertainment options like books, toys, or tablets to keep children occupied during long journeys.

Advise parents to check the car seat requirements and regulations at the destination if planning to rent a car.

15.5 Ensure Health and Safety

Encourage parents to pack a well-stocked travel first aid kit that includes essential medications, band-aids, and antiseptic creams.

Advise checking vaccination requirements and consulting with a pediatrician before traveling to ensure children are up-to-date on immunizations.
Recommend purchasing travel insurance that covers medical emergencies and provides assistance in case of illness or injury.

15.6 Keep Kids Entertained

Provide suggestions for keeping children entertained during travel, such as interactive games, coloring books, or audio books.

Recommend involving children in trip planning by allowing them to choose activities or destinations.
Encourage parents to research child-friendly apps or educational materials that can be used during travel.

15.7 Maintain a Flexible Schedule

Emphasize the importance of maintaining a flexible schedule when traveling with kids to accommodate their needs.

Encourage parents to plan breaks and downtime for children to rest and recharge.

Suggest allowing for spontaneous detours or changes in plans to accommodate children's interests or moods.

15.8 Engage Kids in the Destination

Encourage parents to involve children in learning about the destination's culture, history, and traditions.

Suggest age-appropriate books or documentaries to introduce children to the destination before travel.

Encourage children to interact with locals and participate in cultural activities to enhance their understanding of the place.

15.9 Establish Safety Rules

Advise parents to establish safety rules and guidelines for children during travel, such as holding hands in crowded places or staying close to parents.

Recommend using child locator devices or ID bracelets in busy tourist areas.

Encourage parents to teach children basic phrases in the local language for safety and communication purposes.

15.10 Capture and Cherish Memories

Emphasize the importance of capturing and cherishing family travel memories.

Suggest keeping a travel journal or creating a scrapbook to document experiences.

Encourage parents to involve children in capturing photos or creating travel mementos.

(By including these travel hacks for traveling with kids, the book aims to assist parents in planning and executing enjoyable and

stress-free family vacations, ensuring that the experience is memorable for the entire family.)

A Few Words & Thank You's ♥

I hope that you find this book of travel hacks convenient and beneficial for intermediate and advanced travelers as you plan and go on your ventures across the globe.

I thank you for taking the time to read this book. I wrote the book because of my autism and OCD and for people like me who just like to be prepared and be able to figure out how to make certain things work or do certain things as far as planning, traveling and more!

In this you were able to find hidden easter eggs and cracks in the system to make a trip or vacation a homerun in ways you couldn't imagine or to just make things easier, even if you're on a budget and to be wise doing so all while saving money and time in the process.

So my fellow Wanders, take this book and use it as a tool to get around the globe efficiently, to be wise, smart, safe, aware, ready. I do plan to make more books about hacks and other things so be on the lookout for them!

Hey, I might show you how to time travel but hey I guess only time will tell yeah? Peace and blessing and Wander Wisely .

- *Jaxs, Thank You All* ⚣

- *Photo Credit To UI Visualz*